Believing

IN THE *Future*

Toward a Missiology of
Western Culture

D A V I D   J.   B O S C H

TRINITY PRESS INTERNATIONAL
Valley Forge, Pennsylvania

Gracewing

First U.S. edition
published 1995 by
TRINITY PRESS INTERNATIONAL
P.O. Box 851
Valley Forge, PA 19482-0851
U.S.A.

First British edition
published 1995 by
GRACEWING
2 Southern Avenue
Leominster
Herefordshire HR6 0QF
England

Cover design: Brian Preuss

Library of Congress Cataloging-in-Publication Data
Bosch, David Jacobus.
   Believing in the future : toward a missiology of Western culture /
David J. Bosch. — 1st ed.
      p.   cm. — (Christian mission and modern culture)
   Includes bibliographical references.
   ISBN 1-56338-117-6 (Trinity Press)
   ISBN 0-85244-333-1 (Gracewing)
   1. Missions—Theory.   2. Christianity and culture.   3. Missions—
History.   4. Mission of the church.   I. Title.   II. Series.
BV2063.B648   1995
266'.01—dc20   95-16093
                                                              CIP

Printed by Lightning Source UK Ltd.

95   96   97   98   99   00   6   5   4   3   2   1

Contents

PREFACE TO THE SERIES vii

FOREWORD ix

1. THE "POSTMODERN WORLD" 1

2. THE LEGACY OF THE ENLIGHTENMENT 5

3. THE CHRISTIAN FAITH IN A POSTMODERN AGE . . . 15

4. CONTOURS OF A MISSIOLOGY
   OF WESTERN CULTURE 27

5. THE IMPOSSIBILITY OF NOT BELIEVING 47

6. CONCLUSION 55

NOTES 63

REFERENCES CITED 65

Preface to the Series

Both Christian mission and modern culture, widely regarded as antagonists, are in crisis. The emergence of the
modern mission movement in the early nineteenth century
cannot be understood apart from the rise of technocratic
society. Now, at the end of the twentieth century, both
modern culture and Christian mission face an uncertain
future.

One of the developments integral to modernity was the
way the role of religion in culture was redefined. Whereas
religion had played an authoritative role in the culture of
Christendom, modern culture was highly critical of religion and increasingly secular in its assumptions. A sustained
effort was made to banish religion to the backwaters of
modern culture.

The decade of the 1980s witnessed further momentous
developments on the geopolitical front with the collapse of
communism. In the aftermath of the breakup of the system of power blocs that dominated international relations
for a generation, it is clear that religion has survived even
if its institutionalization has undergone deep change and
its future forms are unclear. Secularism continues to oppose
religion, while technology has emerged as a major source

of power and authority in modern culture. Both confront Christian faith with fundamental questions.

The purpose of this series is to probe these developments from a variety of angles with a view to helping the church understand its missional responsibility to a culture in crisis. One important resource is the church's experience of two centuries of cross-cultural mission that has reshaped the church into a global Christian *ecumene*. The focus of our inquiry will be the church in modern culture. The series (1) examines modern/postmodern culture from a missional point of view; (2) develops the theological agenda that the church in modern culture must address in order to recover its own integrity; and (3) tests fresh conceptualizations of the nature and mission of the church as it engages modern culture. In other words, these volumes are intended to be a forum where conventional assumptions can be challenged and alternative formulations explored.

This series is a project authorized by the Institute of Mennonite Studies, research agency of the Associated Mennonite Biblical Seminary, and supported by a generous grant from the Pew Charitable Trusts.

Editorial Committee

ALAN NEELY
H. WAYNE PIPKIN
WILBERT R. SHENK

Foreword

This volume by David J. Bosch was written in late 1991 in the form of an essay and was presented by him to a group that met in Paris in January 1992 to discuss what steps we might take to develop a missiology of Western culture. In accepting the invitation to participate in the meeting, Bosch indicated that he was feeling a moral obligation to turn his attention to this theme. Although he had only recently completed the writing of his massive work *Transforming Mission* (Orbis Books, 1991), he recognized that he had not yet truly engaged the challenge of modern culture to the gospel. And he sensed this to be a priority concern for our day. Before leaving Paris we discussed possible publication of the essay, and he proposed the title it now bears.

David Bosch's tragic death in an automobile accident April 15, 1992, has left all of us who have known him as a friend, colleague, outstanding mission theologian, and church statesman with a sense of irreparable loss. He combined in his life and ministry first-rate scholarship and devoted Christian discipleship. His loyalty to his native land, South Africa, seemed to be intensified precisely by a personal integrity that required that he live out what he understood the gospel to entail. David Bosch knew existentially, and to a degree most of us never reach, what it means to live and work against the stream of culture — to be countercultural. He was the prophet among us.

Along with his vast knowledge of the field of biblical studies, theology, church history, and missiology, David Bosch had the rare ability to distill the insight and wisdom to meet the demands of the day. His broad sympathies with all parts of the Christian family and his gifts of communication made him a trusted and respected friend wherever he went.

Appreciation is expressed to Mrs. Anne-Marie Bosch for her cooperation in the publication of this volume.

WILBERT R. SHENK

1

The "Postmodern World"

We live in the "post-" era. Since 1958, when Michael Polanyi presented his plea for the development of a "post-critical" and "postmodern" philosophy, the term has been used with increasing frequency. Daniel Bell (1973) and Alain Touraine (1977:155–66) talk about a "postindustrial society." Jürgen Habermas (1988) — like many before him, though in a different manner — defends the idea of a "post-metaphysical" age. Harvey Cox (1984) makes a case for a "postmodern theology," as do several authors in a volume edited by Hans Küng and David Tracy and published in the same year. And in a more recent book, Küng depicts the contemporary world as post-Eurocentric, postcolonial, postimperial, postsocialist, postindustrial, postpatriarchal, postideological, and postconfessional (Küng, 1990:40f).

The "post-" phenomenon is not just a fad. We have truly entered into an epoch fundamentally at variance with anything we have experienced to date. Likewise, there can be no doubt that the new situation is confronting the Christian church with unprecedented challenges. It will be impossible to draw the contours of the new epoch within the confines of this volume. A few generalizations, acting in a sense as *pars pro toto*, will have to suffice.

The dominant characteristics of the contemporary world are its thoroughgoing secular nature and its radical anthropocentricity. And even if Küng calls it "post-Eurocentric," it is still a world in which the West calls the shots — much more so, in fact, after the Gulf War, the collapse of communism, and the demise of the Soviet Union. Even so, the confidence of the 1960s and early 1970s is gone, not only in the Second and Third Worlds, but also in the First. For approximately a decade and a half an unbridled optimism had taken hold of the world and, for that matter, of the Christian church. This was true of mainline Protestantism (think, in this respect, of the 1966 Church and Society Conference in Geneva and the 1968 assembly of the World Council of Churches in Uppsala), of evangelicalism, which experienced a rapid upsurge in this period (compare, for instance, the conferences in Wheaton and Berlin, both in 1966, and the Lausanne Conference of 1974), and of Roman Catholicism, which experienced a massive renewal and *aggiornamento* during the Second Vatican Council and the Medellín Conference of 1968 (for an optimistic portrayal of the future of Catholicism in the wake of the Council, see Rahner 1969:744–59).

Little of this optimism has remained anywhere in the world. I will return to the Third World later. For the moment, I will list just a few characteristics of the contemporary First World. We live, says Touraine (1977), in a "self-producing," "programmed," and "fully administered" society, run by giant industrial corporations under the direction of teams of technocrats. It is a totalitarian society, but its totalitarianism is hardly recognized, for it comes across as benevolent (also Bellah 1991:465–72). Its presuppositions and spin-offs include centralization, bureaucratization, ecological damage, manipulation and exploitation of human beings, relentless consumerism, and chronic unemployment (further aggravated, ironically, by the termination of the Cold War and the arms race!). It is a permissive society, without norms, models, and traditions, an "immediate" society, without past and often without future: people live utterly in the present and seek instant gratification (or, in many parts of the Third World, survival just for today: "We'll see about tomorrow if and when we get there"). At the same time, people in the West are inundated by a veritable deluge of information and entertainment, mainly via television, a circumstance that gives rise not only to shattering pluralism but also to widespread pollution of the mind. The side effects of all of this are mind-boggling. To mention only one example: *The International Herald Tribune* of 12 January 1990 reported that, according to estimates of the National Council on Crime and Delinquency, the United States will, up to 1995, have to spend $35,000,000,000 on the construction of additional prison cells for an estimated total of 460,000 new drug-related offenders (Küng 1990:57). And, menacingly in the background, there looms the specter of AIDS.

All of this and much more has for millions of people created a gap between vision and reality that, in turn, has precipitated a crisis in their worldview and self-understanding. This has not happened at the level of the individual only, but also in respect of entire communities. And when such a crisis involves the dominant visions of a particular society, as is the case today, the entire society is prone to massive breakdown. The very scaffolding on which people are

2

The Legacy of the Enlightenment

It has become customary to blame the present malaise of the West on the Enlightenment. I, too, have supported this thesis (Bosch 1991:262–74). I have suggested that the Enlightenment frame of mind, as it evolved in the course of time, had spawned seven cardinal convictions. First, its emphasis on *reason* suggested that the human mind was the indubitable point of departure for all knowing. Second, it divided all of reality into thinking *subjects* and, over against these, *objects* that could be analyzed and exploited. Third, it dropped all reference to *purpose* and viewed every process only in terms of cause and effect. Fourth, it put a high premium on *progress*, on expansion, advance, and modernization. Fifth, it proceeded from the assumption that all true knowledge was *factual, value-free*, and *neutral*. Over against *facts* there were *values*, which were not objectively true, the holding of which was, therefore, a matter of taste. Religion was, in the course of time, relegated to this category. Sixth, the Enlightenment proceeded from the assumption that *all problems were in principle solvable*. And last, it regarded people as *emancipated, autonomous individuals*, no longer under the tutelage of "superiors."

5

I have suggested, in addition, not only that the Enlightenment has made deep inroads into Western theological thinking (:274–84), but also that virtually the entire modern Western missionary enterprise, particularly its Protestant version, was predicated on Enlightenment assumptions (:284–345).

Early responses to my recent book have indicated that at least some of my readers have detected a fierce anti-Enlightenmentism in my reasoning in spite of the qualifications I have made in this respect (:360f). In this volume I want to add several more qualifications, because I want to make my indebtedness to the Enlightenment very clear.

First, it should be stated explicitly that we cannot isolate the Enlightenment as being solely responsible for what has led up to the contemporary situation. In a sense, the modern worldview was but the logical consummation of a way of thinking the roots of which lay far back in Greek antiquity, whence it penetrated Christian thinking. Since the third century C.E. the belief that God was self-revealed to humankind in two books (the Book of Revelation, made accessible by faith, and the Book of Nature, made accessible by observation and the faculty of reason) was part and parcel of the Christian tradition. Revelation and science were, however, not competing epistemological domains; rather, they were complementary and harmonious. Originally, of course, there was a clear subordination of the latter to the former: science was the "handmaiden" (*ancilla*) to theology, the "queen of the sciences." Gradually this subservient role of science and nature would come under pressure. As early as the fourth century, in the writings of Augustine (Kaiser 1991:21f, 34), we can detect the first clear indication of the idea of the autonomy of nature that was to prevail in the West after the seventeenth century. In respect of the *economy*, the gulf between God and the world opened by Augustine was widened as early as the thirteenth century (with the rise of capitalism and the disregard of the canonical prohibitions against charging interest); and in respect of the other sciences, in the fourteenth and fifteenth centuries (Guardini 1950:37f) — all of this well before the onset of the Enlightenment.

The Enlightenment, then, was really a symptom of a much more fundamental problem that was, in a very real sense, inherent in the Christian faith itself and in its encounter with the world. It is, as such, our inescapable legacy (Hoedemaker 1990:59f).

Second, it is important to keep in mind that the fathers of the Enlightenment were all Christians; they viewed what they did and said as service to God. This was true, for instance, of Francis Bacon (1561–1626), Galileo Galilei (1564–1642), René Descartes (1596–1650), John Locke (1632–1704), Isaac Newton (1642–1727), and Gottfried Wilhelm Leibniz (1646–1716), to mention but a few (for details, see Kaiser 1991). Descartes, for instance, who is generally regarded as the father of the Enlightenment, was deeply rooted in scholastic theology (Kaiser 1991:161–68). Leibniz stood in the seventeenth century spiritualist tradition and viewed his work as exalting God's wisdom and power (:158–61). In his reflections on science, Bacon, the English Puritan, followed John Calvin (:122, 146–48). Newton, who was both a mathematician and a biblical scholar, sought to formulate a natural philosophy that would preserve the role of God in the cosmos and vindicate the Faith (:178–86). And so we could go on.

Third, it may be helpful to keep in mind that the Enlightenment evolved differently in different countries and that, perhaps, this circumstance accounts for variations that might even today be detected in these countries and their peoples.

In France, because of the peculiar sociopolitical circumstances in the eighteenth century, the Cartesian tradition soon became mechanistic and atheistic. Still, there has continued, side by side with the Cartesian tradition, a Pascalian tradition, so much so that Allan Bloom (1987:52) can say that "every Frenchman is born, or at least early on becomes, Cartesian or Pascalian." He adds, "Descartes and Pascal represent a choice between reason and revelation, science and piety, the choice from which everything else follows" (ibid.).

In England, on the contrary, there never was such a persistent and irreconcilable quarrel between the secular and the religious. Natural science and revelation were not regarded as competing epistemological domains. John Locke, for instance, insisted that theology cannot be at odds with science, for revelation, on which theology was based, is nothing less than an exalted form of science (Becker 1991: 142). When this view increasingly came under pressure, the solution was not as in France found in atheism, but in Deism. In this model, natural theology was elevated as the first and independent section of theology, leaving revealed religion as questionable adjunct (:143), a role model that was, apparently, also adopted in the Netherlands, where it culminated, in 1876, in the *duplex ordo* arrangement at state universities.

Germany, by contrast, remained outside the mainstream of Enlightenment thinking until the early decades of the eighteenth century, when the ideas of Leibniz were popularized (:143). This led, however, to a fierce controversy, centered on the person of Christian Wolff, who taught mathematics, physics, and philosophy at the University of Halle, the stronghold of Pietism and of August Hermann Francke (Becker:passim). Wolff followed Leibniz rather than Newton, and viewed the world as a kind of perfect clock or a machine that was not in need of further correction; he could therefore assert, "In the sciences, one is not allowed recourse to the will of God" (:147). In the ensuing controversy, which led to the expulsion of Wolff in 1723, Pietists and orthodox Lutherans made common cause against the mechanistic conception of Wolff and others, a circumstance that seems to have dominated the German scholarly scene for a very long time. Wolff may, incidentally, also be credited with giving an early impetus to the developments of the social sciences and the application of a "scientific" approach to the humanities (ibid.).

In the United States, the situation was different again, as West (1991), Hunsberger (1991), Hauerwas and Willimon (1989, 1991), and Bellah (1985, 1991) have cogently argued. Unlike the European countries I have discussed, religion was disestablished with the birth of the new nation. On the surface, this should have led to an even fiercer antagonism between religion and science than was the case in Europe. Strangely, however, it did not happen. To this day, Americans are far more religious than their European counterparts. One reason for this may, in fact, lie precisely in the constitutional separation between religion and the state, as enshrined in the First Amendment ("Congress shall make no law respecting an establishment of religion, or prohibiting the free exercise thereof"). Other reasons may be that the ethos of the Puritan founders still persists, even if in a thoroughly watered-down form, and that the Enlightenment arrived rather late on the North American scene. Yet another reason, at a more profound level, may lie in the pervasive influence of the philosophy of John Locke on the United States (see Bellah 1991). On the surface, this philosophy looked so thoroughly Christian (read: Protestant), not least because it unconditionally endorsed the Protestant tenet that individual believers themselves could interpret the will of God. On the national level, the Lockean philosophy spawned the kind of civil religion classically encapsulated in President Bush's call, early in 1991, for a national day of prayer concerning the war with Iraq (Hauerwas and Willimon 1991:421f quote the text).[1] This is not only a Protestant phenomenon, however; as a matter of fact, much of civil religion is also in evidence in American Catholicism, if sometimes for other reasons, as Grindel (1991: 39–101) has shown.

Of course, since the late eighteenth century the influence of the Enlightenment tended to "level out" the earlier differences between the various countries. Even so, some of those differences have survived to this day, even if they are well concealed. We should keep this in mind when we talk about a "missiology of Western culture." It cannot be the same for all countries of the West.

Fourth, it should not be forgotten that the more thoroughgoing, rationalist, and mechanist thrust of the Enlightenment was really never, at any point, left unchallenged. At the beginning of the seventeenth century, three fairly distinct currents of scientific research, each boasting an ancient tradition, were vying for supremacy. It is not easy to put labels to them, for different terms were used in different periods, quite apart from the fact that the three traditions cross-fertilized each other. Broadly speaking, then, they were (1) the organicist tradition, based on the work of Aristotle, the dominant metaphor of which was the organism and which emphasized wholeness and interdependence; (2) the hermetic-cabalist, "occult," alchemical, or spiritualist tradition, according to which knowledge would come only via mystical illumination; and (3) the mechanist tradition, which revived the science and mathematics of Archimedes with its machine analogies (Kaiser 1991:101–7, 150–61; Leegwater 1991:passim). In addition to appealing to ancient authorities for support, all three incorporated religious assumptions about the universe. By the end of the seventeenth century, however, the mechanist tradition, in the guise of a new mechanical and rationalist philosophy, had triumphed.

This did not spell the end of the other two traditions, however. The cabalist tradition, for instance, survives to this day in the form of various parasciences, several of which have gained widespread recognition (for examples, see Eberlein 1991:541). The organicist tradition staged several comebacks, for instance in German Idealism and Romanticism (compare, for instance, Romantic *Naturphilosophie*, and the poetry of Goethe). Various other protests against the rationalism of the mechanistic tradition and against its tendency to interpret facts as value-free and the same for all were staged, albeit often unintentionally, by scholars as different from one another as G. W. F. Hegel, Ludwig Feuerbach, Karl Marx, and Sigmund Freud. Such protests need not lead to pure historicism (Baum 1979: 231–54), to the anarchist and subjectivist approach to science advocated by Paul Feyerabend (1975; also Chalmers 1985:134–45), or to the irrationalism of postmodernists in the tradition of a Jean-François Lyotard (1986; also Baum 1991). One may, for instance, refer to twentieth century philosophical schools that have, with varying degrees of success, staged a true alternative to the positivism of the High Enlightenment tradition without lapsing into this kind of relativism: the Critical Theory of the Frankfurt School, Critical Realism, Critical Hermeneutics (Nel 1989), Systems Thinking (Fensham 1990), and the like. In addition, it is common knowledge that the work of Albert Einstein and Niels Bohr has profoundly challenged the very foundations on which the mechanist and rationalist tradition stand.

Fifth, the Enlightenment also brought with it profoundly positive elements without which we would have been incomparably poorer. Even Polanyi, one of the fiercest critics of Enlightenment rationalism, recognized this. He says, "The critical movement . . . was perhaps the most fruitful effort ever sustained by the human mind" (Polanyi 1958: 265), and adds that the past few centuries "have enriched us mentally and morally to an extent unrivalled by any period of similar duration" (:266). We should, in fact, "be grateful for the prolonged attacks made by rationalists on religion for forcing us to renew the ground of the Christian faith" (:286). This is both a blessing and an affliction or a challenge. Our greatly increased critical powers, he says

> have endowed our mind with a capacity of self-transcendence of which we can never again divest ourselves. We have plucked from the Tree a second apple which has for ever imperiled our knowledge of Good and Evil, and we must learn to know these

qualities hence-forth in the blinding light of our new analytical powers (:268).

Newbigin (1986:43), another astute critic of the Enlightenment, concurs: "The 'light' in the Enlightenment was real light." It would therefore be foolish to hanker nostalgically for the pre-Enlightenment worldview and world order. It would be equally absurd to exchange Enlightenment rationalism for the irrationalism that we encounter in some branches of postmodernism (Feyerabend, Lyotard, etc.). This hostility toward reason, which seems indeed to suggest that any form of human dialogue and mutual intelligibility is unattainable, cannot but lead to a total breakdown in interhuman communication and ultimately to chaos.

It is therefore to be affirmed emphatically that the process leading up to the Enlightenment and the Enlightenment itself were also a blessing. It was not simply a case of a "disaster" having hit the church. It is an oversimplification to juxtapose Enlightenment and Christian faith as if they must be implacable foes. Therefore the solution does not lie merely in turning the clock back and insisting that, come what may, we just have to learn to believe again (Hoedemaker 1990:60f).

3

The Christian Faith in a Postmodern Age

Even so, it cannot be denied that the Enlightenment has had a far-reaching impact on the Christian faith, particularly in the West. The secularization that followed in its wake is a permanent thorn in the flesh of the church, and we can no longer presuppose or postulate a society in which this problem does not exist (Hoedemaker 1990:63). Since the seventeenth century more and more people have discovered, originally to their surprise, that they could ignore God and the church, yet be none the worse for it. It would seem that Catholicism (and, for that matter, [Eastern] Orthodoxy) has succeeded better than Protestantism in withstanding the erosive impact of the Enlightenment. Several reasons, particularly sociological ones, may be advanced to explain this. Perhaps, however, there may be a basic theological reason for this as well, one to which Hans Küng refers (without, necessarily, drawing from it the conclusions I will now draw). Küng (1987:222–33; also Sölle 1990:9–11) suggests that, fundamental to medieval scholastic theology (and, to some extent, to all subsequent Catholic theological thinking), there is a harmonious scheme of nature and supernature in which everything fits a position

classically formulated by Thomas of Aquinas. The scheme
is something like the following:

Faith (Mystery)	Grace	Church (Pope)	Theology	the Christian
Reason	Nature	State (Emperor)	Philosophy	the Human

If one now looks at this outline from the perspective of
H. Richard Niebuhr's *Christ and Culture* (1956), it would
appear that Catholic theology has a proclivity toward the
model Niebuhr identifies as "Christ *above* culture." This position can, however, also lead to the adoption of Niebuhr's
model of "the Christ of culture" (Sölle 1990:10).[2] In neither
of the two models is there a fundamentally unresolvable
conflict between Christ and culture or, if one wishes, between faith and reason. In the first model, faith reigns
supreme over reason; in the second, faith and reason are
no longer clearly distinguished. In neither of these two
instances did this, of necessity, involve abiding hostility
between the Christian faith and science.

It was essentially different in Protestantism, however.
The Reformation represented a fundamental break with the
Thomistic synthesis and replaced it with a model character-
ized by a radical diastasis:

$$
\begin{array}{ccc}
\text{Faith} & \Longleftrightarrow & \text{Reason} \\
\text{Grace} & \Longleftrightarrow & \text{Nature} \\
\text{Church} & \Longleftrightarrow & \text{World} \\
\text{Theology} & \Longleftrightarrow & \text{Philosophy} \\
\text{The Christian} & \Longleftrightarrow & \text{The Human} \\
+ & & -
\end{array}
$$

In this model, reason, nature, the world, and philosophy are judged *negatively* (hence the minus), whereas faith, grace, the church, and theology are evaluated *positively.* Looked at from the perspective of Niebuhr's taxonomy, this suggests a position of "Christ *against* culture" or, at the very least, "Christ and culture *in paradox.*" This introduced into Protestantism the idea of an abiding incompatibility between church and world — what Tillich (1951:237–59) referred to as the "Protestant principle." Of course, some manifestations of Protestant theology (notably the "liberal" tradition) closely approximated the "Christ of culture" position, but even where this happened, elements of antithesis or diastasis usually remained. Only rarely was the "Protestant principle" completely surrendered: very few theologians ever subscribed to Kant's idea of locating theology only within the limits of reason or confining it merely to "practical reason."[3]

Even so, virtually all of Protestant theology, whether conservative or progressive, succumbed to the pressures of the Enlightenment to make faith rationally plausible. Its main interlocutor, since the Enlightenment, has been philosophy, and its overall purpose was to make religion acceptable to its cultured despisers, à la Schleiermacher. One of the ways in which Schleiermacher attempted to safeguard theology and religion was to define it as something done by professionals for the sake of the believing community. The pastor became a professional on a par with other professionals: physicians, teachers, lawyers, and so on. However, because of the "Christ against culture" substratum in Protestantism, this came to mean that believers had to commute between different plausibility structures: when in church, their plausibility structure was determined by the

Christian faith; when in the factory or surgery, it was determined by the mechanistic paradigm. The first plausibility structure was not allowed to challenge the second, for it belonged to another order.

In the course of time this led to a dichotomy of two completely different and unrelated worlds (Guardini 1950: 100). It is not that the new worldview publicly opposed religion or proscribed it (although this did, of course, happen in some Communist countries); rather, it fostered a private religion that had no real function in society as a whole (Cox 1984:12). And the underlying "Christ against culture" stance in Protestantism meant, in practice, that religion was relegated to the private sector, to the world of values, where people are free to choose what they like. Thus, where religion did persist, it had to settle for a much reduced place in the sun. Everything else is autonomous, and religion has nothing to do with it. In this climate, theology could only justify its existence in universities if it adopted the same scientific precepts and methods as all the other disciplines that were no longer under the tutelage of the church. In theology, as in the other disciplines, one had to have "the courage to make use of one's own understanding" (Kant). Religion lost the function it had in an earlier era — that of explaining the world.

In spite of this, Western society continues to draw parasitically on the Christian faith. It is impossible to erase this tradition or to undo the Christian legacy, as people are now also discovering in the former Socialist countries. If contemporary Western human beings become pagans, says Guardini (1950:108f), they will be pagans in a manner fundamentally different from pre-Christian paganism.[4] There is, in this respect, a peculiar ambiguity in the West: on

the one hand the Christian tradition is studiously ignored;
on the other, Christianity's accomplishments are laid claim
to, almost as if they belong to everybody (Guardini 1950:
112). Many values that are simply taken for granted as being part and parcel of the modern Enlightenment world are,
however, actually deeply rooted in Judaeo-Christianity. The
moral commandments of the Decalogue are, for instance,
accepted as ethical bases in the majority of democra-
cies (Vanackere 1990:107). Even Marxism is manifestly a
Judaeo-Christian heresy.

A bizarre case of the modern world continuing to draw
on its Christian past is the way the Grand Ideologies
(Lübbe 1986: *"Hochideologien"*) of the twentieth century
(Marxism, Fascism, National Socialism) have usurped the
position of the Christian faith (Lübbe 1986:53–73). On
the one hand they purport to be consistently scientific, in
the Enlightenment definition of the term. This is particularly true of dialectical materialism,[5] but also of racism.[6]
They claim to be objectively true. It thus follows that
ideologies become possible only because of Enlightenment scientism and that they stand in the tradition of
the criticism of religion, as this evolved in the nineteenth
century.

On the other hand, however, the Grand Ideologies con-
tain all the attributes of religion. They play the role that
religion used to play. Therefore, in extreme cases (as, until
recently, in Albania) this may even lead to the proscrip-
tion of any religion and religious activity. Ideologies are
therefore, simultaneously, anti-religion *and* pseudo- or ersatz religions.[7] They can, under certain circumstances, become extremely doctrinaire, resembling anti-Enlightenment
religious fundamentalism rather than Enlightenment con-

descension toward firmly held beliefs. They may have canonical texts, prophets, messianic personalities, confessions of faith, offices, martyrs, and elaborate eschatologies, and they can be as intolerant of "unorthodox" views as the most fanatic religionists are. Sometimes, of course, they can become even more sinister, for instance when they arrogate the Christian faith to their ideology. This is, for instance, what happened in National Socialism (for references, see Lübbe 1986:57, note 10) and still happens in the case of the protagonists of extreme nationalism and racism, in South Africa and elsewhere.

Küng (1990:41, 68) suggests that we have now moved into a *post*-ideological era. Whether this is indeed true remains to be seen. Perhaps we will indeed, for the time being, not have to contend with anything like the classic Grand Ideologies; however, we will continue to encounter "soft" ideologies. I am referring to those ideologies that can perhaps only with difficulty be recognized as ideologies: the "American Way of Life," the "New World Order," the "Free Market System," and the like (Bellah 1991:465–72). Most of these ideologies, which often come to us in the guise of "civil religion," look thoroughly "Christian" and therefore completely harmless to the Christian faith.

In a sense, then, the Grand Ideologies betray something fundamental about religion within the setting of the modern, scientistic world. On the one hand one encounters, in Enlightenment rationalism, an almost fanatically intolerant attitude toward any convictions that appear to dispute the orthodoxy of the so-called scientific worldview. The aim is to arrive at a residue of knowledge that is completely determined by objectively true evidence, so that we may gain "for ourselves a possession which can never again be contested"

(Kant, quoted by Polanyi 1958:270). In this view there would eventually, after the dark ages of theology and meta-physical speculation, emerge positive, indubitable scientific knowledge (Bernstein 1985:5). This dogmatism, however, aims at being "user-friendly": it is for the express benefit of all humanity. Increased and incontestable knowledge about the natural order, society, and politics, so the argument goes, will spontaneously lead to the intelligent formulation of policies and projects that will ameliorate social inequity and injustice and enable us to solve all the problems of society — indeed, of the world (:xii). It is hoped, more-over, that the social sciences would, in the course of time, reach the same precision as the natural sciences, which have been so manifestly vindicated by the technological progress they had brought about. This could, however, happen only when and if people cease to take recourse to religion: the social and natural sciences are completely autonomous and find their point of reference within themselves. People are to surmount their feeling of dependence and become to-tal masters of their destiny. Inherent in the worldview of the Enlightenment there lurks a "fantasy of omnipotence" (Vanackere 1990:106).

There is, then, a declared intolerance in Enlightenment scientism. This has, however, its corollary in an equally pro-nounced relativism. Sometimes this relativism exists side by side with dogmatism — the former operative in respect of "values," the latter in respect of "facts." Because there are no universal norms, people may live and do as they please. All kinds of lifestyles are in order; there is no enemy other than the one who is not open to everything; indiscriminateness is the overriding moral imperative, the basic thesis argued by Bloom (1987). We live in a do-it-yourself world, in a supermarket where the choice is limitless and determined solely by personal preference. The philosophy behind this is, "Since there is no absolute value, I consider all values to be equally unimportant," or, "Since there is more than one value, I appreciate all values equally" — two positions that, in any case, boil down to the same (*pace* Eberlein 1991:543). At other times, however, the relativist view is extended also to the area traditionally reserved for science or indubitable "facts." This happens, for instance, in the anarchistic theory of knowledge of Paul Feyerabend (1975) and in some branches of poststructuralism, deconstructionism, and postmodernism. For Lyotard, for instance, because there is no metatruth, everything becomes arbitrary; he writes (1986:xxiv): "I define 'postmodern' as incredulity toward meta-narratives."[8]

Both dogmatic scientism and extreme relativism had disastrous consequences. In one case the point of departure was the utter reliability of unaided reason; in the other it was personal preference or experience. In both instances it was purely self-referential; its criteria were immanent. Both models celebrated freedom; but people were unprepared for the freedom they have arrogated to themselves: they cannot handle it. And because they have no point of reference beyond themselves, they can be subjugated by other human beings, exploited and manipulated. It is therefore typical of the modern world that people (individuals and, indeed, entire groups and nations) are often used as objects. Writing in the wake of the horrors of World War II and of Nazism, Guardini says:

> All these terrible things surely did not just fall from heaven or, more precisely, rise up from hell! All the

incomprehensible systems of degradation and destruc-
tion were not just invented after everything had been
in order previously. Such monstrosities surely cannot
just be ascribed to degenerated individuals or small
groups; they derive from perversions and contamina-
tions that have been at work for a very long time.
Whatever may be termed moral norm, responsibility,
honor, alertness of conscience, cannot just disappear
from the totality of life, unless it has been corrupted
long ago already (1950:90f; my translation).

In this paradigm, then, there is nothing that prevents
politics from becoming a mere game in which power and
self-interest reign supreme, economy from being determined solely by exploitation for one's own benefit, nature
from being treated as mere object for our experiments, and
technology from being merely cold and utilitarian.

The illusion that human hopes for freedom, justice, and
true progress can be realized by relying on reason or human
resolve alone, or by the mechanics of economic, technological, or political development, has finally exploded.
Enlightenment reason, which had declared itself autonomous and had conferred legitimacy on itself, is now being
challenged to defend its legitimacy. But this cannot do, for
a rational process left to itself resembles a self-propelling
machine the functioning of which no longer stands under
the control of a purpose. The "authorities" try to curb
the excesses unleashed by rudderless rationalism or unbridled relativism by making laws to keep things in check;
but, as an ancient Roman adage has it, *Quid leges sine
moribus?* — What are laws without morals? And morals
so essential for the survival of the human race cannot

be generated by a worldview that has no referent outside itself.

By and large, in our own time, people have begun to give up the expectations of the Enlightenment; yet they still hold on to its premise — particularly the idea that reason is the ultimate arbitrator. In *Dialektik der Aufklärung* (1947), Horkheimer and Adorno argue, for instance, that the Enlightenment and modern science, which lie at the base of the modern, rationalized society, have miscarried. They acknowledge that Enlightenment rationality has been self-destructive and that its "instrumental reason" is fundamentally corrupted. And yet they refuse to surrender what they call their *petitio principii:* human reason as point of departure. Even Jürgen Habermas (1988), in spite of all his criticism of his two older colleagues, does not relinquish this *petitio principii;* he merely reinterprets it and wants to use it to guide the "modern project" to an appropriate end. This must happen on the basis of modernity's own principles, particularly human reason. Habermas's notion of rationality is broader than that of Horkheimer and Adorno, but it is still left to its own resources and finds its ultimate criterion in itself. This reveals a fundamental problem in much so-called postmodern philosophy: on the one hand the autonomy of reason is rejected; on the other this is done solely by means of reason. But, in Küng's words (1990:45), "Reason simply cannot be cured by reason itself" (*"Die Vernunft läßt sich nun einmal nicht einfach durch Vernunft sanieren"*).

It would therefore seem, as Guardini (1950:84–86) puts it, that the culture of the modern era has misunderstood the human being, not just in part, but fundamentally and totally; neither positivism, materialism, idealism, existentialism, nor any of the other more recent philosophical schools can comprehend what humanity really is. If we want to grasp that, we have to move beyond human reason and Enlightenment scientism.

4

Contours of a Missiology of Western Culture

I have attempted to give just a small glimpse of what contemporary Western culture is like and of its profound malaise. My excursus has intimated, albeit inadequately, what we are up against when we talk about designing a "missiology of Western culture." To this I now turn. I will proceed by indicating some dimensions and ingredients that, I suggest, have to be included in such a missiology.

Toward a Missionary Theology

Some years ago the editor of the *Indian Missiological Review* prepared an issue of his journal in which the current situation in the area of missiology in each of the continents would be reflected. He asked me to write an article on missiology in Africa. As I worked through the material, I discovered, increasingly, that it was impossible to distinguish between African *theology* and African *missiology,* that African theology was, to a significant extent, missiological through and through (Bosch 1984:106–8). Johannes Aagaard (1982:266) says the same of Asia: "In Asia theology has to some extent become missiology, while at the same time missiology has become theology. It is probably the most important thing which has happened in the Asian churches."

In the West the situation is manifestly different, as Shenk (1991) has shown. For many centuries Westerners had lived in the climate of Christendom, which operated on the basis of a symbiosis between church and society and in which there were, officially, no nonbelievers. What Stephen Neill (1968:75) says regarding the understanding of the church in England during this period could be said of the church in any country in Europe: it called up "the vision of a typical English village of not more than 400 inhabitants, where all are baptized Christians, compelled to live more or less Christian lives under the brooding eye of parson and squire." In such a context, Neill adds, " 'evangelization' has hardly any meaning, since all are in some sense already Christian, and need no more than to be safeguarded against error in religion and viciousness in life."

The study of theology in this period reveals the same mentality, particularly as it was "reformed" and standardized by F. D. E. Schleiermacher. He established the "fourfold pattern" in theological education, namely, the disciplines of biblical studies, church history, systematic theology, and practical (or pastoral) theology (Farley 1983:74–80; 99–149). In this division, the first three disciplines represented *theory*, the fourth *practice*. With the collapse of Christendom and the disentanglement of society and church, this did not change. Rather, the pattern was reinforced. Practical theology in particular became in the classical definition of Karl Rahner (1966:50) "the theological, normative discipline of the self-realization of the church in all its dimensions" (a view critiqued by Mette 1990:421–23). In this model, then, practical theology was limited to the church and its "self-realization," for which the other theological disciplines had to provide the "theoretical" substructure.

It is clear, in this paradigm, that theology has no interest in the world outside the church, except insofar as the church might wrest "territory" from the world and incorporate this into the church. As a matter of fact, when the modern Western foreign missionary enterprise was initiated, this is how mission was understood, to a significant extent: chunks of the "pagan" world outside Europe had to be conquered and incorporated into Christendom, or, at the very least, into the Christian church. It is interesting to note that the word *mission*, in its modern sense, was first used in the sixteenth century by Jesuits in Northern Germany to refer to their work of reconverting Protestants to Catholicism.

When it became clear that the church also had to do something about the growing numbers of Westerners who had, practically, turned their backs on the Christian faith, this enterprise was referred to as "home missions" (in the English-speaking world) or *"Innere Mission"* (in Germany here, however, the emphasis was on diaconal work rather than on reconversion). Gradually, however, a change of terminology was introduced: "mission" was now used only in respect of work in traditional "non-Christian" countries. Reconversion work in the West was referred to as "evangelism" (or "evangelization"). The latter was judged to be *theologically* different from the former. Margull (1962:275–78; also Verkuyl 1978) defines mission as proclaiming the gospel "where no church as yet exists, where the Lordship of God has never yet historically been proclaimed, where *pagans* are the object of concern," and evangelism as preach-

ing to those who have left the church or who are living in a
post-Christian milieu, such as Eastern Europe.

This view is still widely held, in Protestant as well as Roman Catholic circles, and it is usually linked to the view
that "mission," "out there," is more important than "evangelism," here in the West. A recent example is John Paul II's
missionary encyclical, *Redemptoris Missio* (released on 7 De-
cember 1990), which states in paragraph 32: "Care must
be taken to avoid the risk of putting very different situa-
tions on the same level and of reducing, or even eliminating,
the Church's mission *ad gentes.*" In paragraph 34 the Pope
maintains that the mission *ad gentes* is "missionary activity
proper" (emphasis added); it "is distinct from other ecclesial
activities" and "the first task of the Church."

Of course, the Pope also refers to "new evangelization"
or "reevangelization" in the West. But in this encyclical it is
decidedly underemphasized. And where the Pope does refer to it, it seems to signify, primarily, a desire to effect a
restoration of lost influence in an institutional-ecclesiastical
sense. It is the same thinking we encounter in Protestantism: the notion that, when we discover that the church is
losing influence and members, we had better resign ourselves to an evangelistic campaign in an attempt to redress
the balance, reclaim lost ground, and re-recruit people into
a cultic community that is aligned chiefly on their individual
salvation and their pastoral care.

Mission, in contrast to evangelism, has in the course of
the twentieth century acquired a far richer meaning. But
very few theologians and church leaders employ it with
reference to the situation in the West. It was therefore a
pleasant surprise to meet, in Wilbert Shenk's recent article,
the Birmingham Canon Walter Hobhouse who, as far back

as 1909, argued that "the Church should recognize . . . that she is in reality a missionary Church, not only in heathen lands . . . but in every country" (quoted in Shenk 1991:104). Leaders like Hobhouse remained a minority voice, however. As late as 1943 — when Godin and Daniel published their *France, pays de mission?* in which they argued that France, "the eldest daughter of the Church," had again become a mission field and that a missionary enterprise comparable to what the Catholic Church had undertaken overseas was called for — their reflections were greeted with shock rather than endorsement.

Yet, as far as I can gather on the basis of Shenk's article, neither Hobhouse nor Godin and Daniel went far enough. They merely attacked the geographical myth that mission had to do only with distant countries, but continued to define mission in terms similar to those in which their contemporaries defined evangelism. To the concept of mission as first preaching the gospel to pagans they simply added the notion of mission as the reintroduction of the gospel to neo-pagans. This meant that they continued to perceive mission in terms of its *addresses*, not of its very *nature*, and suggested that mission was accomplished once the gospel has been (re)introduced to a group of people. The same, I fear, was largely true of the report of the 1918 English Archbishops' "Committee of Enquiry into the Evangelistic Work of the Church" (Church of England 1918) and of the British "Nationwide Initiative in Evangelism," (British Council of Churches 1980), which published its report in 1980.

In this definition, then, mission continues to belong to the *adiaphora*, not to the essence of the church. It remains a contingent activity — contingent, that is, on the kind of situation to which Hobhouse and Godin and Daniel had referred or the situation that obtains in those countries where the church is not yet firmly established. It remains peripheral, just as the discipline of missiology remains peripheral, in Western European institutions: only those interested in "overseas" work or in exotic theologies take these courses.

This is, however, decidedly *not* what mission is and what missiology should be involved in. As those Third World missiologies to which I have alluded illustrate, mission refers to a permanent and intrinsic dimension of the church's life. The church "is missionary by its very nature," as the Vatican II Decree on Mission (paragraph 9) put it, and it is impossible to talk about church without at the same time talking about mission. Because God is a missionary God, God's people are missionary people. The church's mission is not secondary to its being; the church exists in being sent and in building up itself for its mission (Barth 1956:725. I am here following the German original rather than the English translation). As Hoedemaker (1988:169–71, 178f) rightly argues, this means that ecclesiology does not precede missiology; there cannot be church without an intrinsic missionary dimension. And Shenk (1991:107) quotes Emil Brunner's famous adage: "The church exists by mission, just as fire exists by burning."

Unless the church of the West begins to understand this, and unless we develop a missionary theology, not just a theology of mission, we will not achieve more than merely patch up the church. We are in need of a missiological agenda for theology, not just a theological agenda for mission; for theology, rightly understood, has no reason to exist other than critically to accompany the *missio Dei* (see, on this, Bosch 1991:489–98).

Mission as Social Ethics

From this fundamental perspective several others follow. The first has to do with our understanding of mission and missiology as they relate to the society in which we find ourselves. Mission is more than and different from recruitment to our brand of religion; it is alerting people to the universal reign of God.

In respect of their relationship to society, Christians have always been tempted to follow one of two ways, both of which are to be excluded if we think of a missiology of Western culture.

The first was to undertake the establishment of a Christian society. For more than a thousand years such a society existed throughout virtually all of Europe. This process of domesticating Christianity already began before Constantine, when Christian apologists attempted to make Christianity acceptable in the Roman Empire by arguing that Christians make exemplary and virtuous citizens.

The idea of instituting a Christian society is, however, untenable, even if only because, in the final analysis, such a religio-political synthesis (Niebuhr's "Christ *of* culture" model) makes it impossible for Christians to adopt a missionary stance vis-à-vis their society. The Christian faith is in this respect different from Islam, which has no theory for distinguishing between religion and the state and no separation between civil rights and religious law: the *sharia* controls a single society, political *and* religious. In any event, reestablishing a Christian society is hardly a viable option in the West; it is, at most, a fantasy of the "Religious Right."

It is the second temptation that is far more real — that

of withdrawing from public life altogether. As our concern over rampant secularization increases, we may in fashioning a missiology of Western culture easily be seduced into concentrating on the "religious" aspect only, leaving the rest to the secular powers, not least because these powers exert massive pressures on the church to limit itself to the soul of the individual. This is, after all, in keeping with the Enlightenment worldview: religion is a private affair, its truth claims are relative and have no place in the public sphere of "facts." But Christian theology itself also contributed to this notion, as it increasingly individualized, interiorized, ecclesiasticized, and privatized salvation.

We will have to do our utmost to resist this temptation. It belongs to our missionary mandate to ask questions about the use of power in our societies, to unmask those that destroy life, to show concern for the victims of society while at the same time calling to repentance those who have turned them into victims, and to articulate God's active wrath against all that distorts and diminishes human beings and all that exploits, squanders, and disfigures the world for selfishness, greed, and self-centered power. Christianity, says Nicholas Wolterstorff (1983:3–22), is not an *avertive* religion but a *world-formative* religion. This is also true of Christian mission, which Berkhof (1966:81–100) calls "a history-making force." It follows that missiology, also in the West, needs to go hand in hand with social and political ethics. As we call people (back) to faith in God through Jesus Christ, we must help them to articulate an answer to the question "What do we have to become Christians *for?*" At least part of the answer to this question will have to be: "In order to be enlisted into God's ministry of reconciliation, peace, and justice on earth." It should be natural for

Christians to be committed to these values. In a sense, as I will argue below, there is already very much religion and believing in Western society. What we do not need, then, is to introduce more religion. The issue is not to talk more about God in a culture that has become irreligious, but how to express, ethically, the coming of God's reign, how to help people respond to the real questions of their context, how to break with the paradigm according to which religion has to do only with the private sphere (Hoedemaker 1990:59, 63f).

This is not to suggest that we will build God's kingdom on earth. It is not ours to inaugurate, but we can help make it more visible, more tangible; we can initiate approximations of God's coming reign. That reign itself is, however, always beyond human utopias. In the end, it will not be built by human hands, not even by Christian hands, but will be divinely bestowed upon us. And yet, even if, in the words of 1 Corinthians 7:29–32, we live in this world "as though" we are not of it, we may under no circumstances flee from it. We are in it, says Shenk, drawing on a biblical image, as "resident aliens," which implies no call to quietism but, rather, to existing in "missionary encounter with the world" (Shenk 1991:109), while knowing that "no socio-political system can ever adequately and fully embody the new order of God's reign" (:106).

Western Mission and the Third World

If a missiology of Western culture cannot ignore the socio-political issues of its own context, neither can it ignore the Third World.

I have already given one reason for this — the fact that

Third World theologies are *missionary* theologies, whereas First World theologies are not. Many Third World Christians seem to realize that they live in a missionary situation, in the fullest sense of the word. Perhaps this is so, first, because the poles between which those theologies move are not those of belief and unbelief or theism and atheism, but rather those of life and death or God (of life) and idols (of death) (Mette 1990:426); and second, because those theologies have, to a significant extent, succeeded in bridging the divide between orthodoxy and orthopraxis, so widespread in Western theology. They are also often, but by no means always, theologies of the people, not, as in the West, the property of an elitist intellectual guild. Because of these and other reasons, Third World theologies may become a force of renewal in the West as we grope toward a missiology of Western culture.

There is a second important reason for including the Third World when we wish to talk missiologically about the West: it is the West's, including Western churches', complicity in respect of the plight of the Third World, together with the growing awareness, in the contemporary world, that solidarity is indivisible.

It is necessary to emphasize this dimension particularly at the present moment, on the eve of the formation of a new European economic and political power block. Already there is talk of the new Europe becoming a "bulwark of affluence against the Third World" (see the title of Müller 1990), of a new "iron curtain" going up between North and South and replacing the one between West and East. Westerners live in a world in which millions of people enjoy a standard of material wealth that few kings and queens could have matched two centuries ago (Newbigin 1986:110), and increasingly Western Christians are not only taking this for granted but finding theological justification for a situation in which the gulf between the rich minority and the abjectly poor majority is widening daily. From 1980 to 1988 the Western industrial nations and Japan, which together have 16 percent of the world's population, have increased their share of the world's gross production from 64.8 to 72.7 percent. In the same period the share of the developing nations has dropped from 22.9 to 15.6 percent, while their share of the world's population increased to 76 percent. Almost a billion people (one-fifth of the world's population) live in absolute poverty. Daily 40,000 children die of famine and related causes (Müller 1990:508). Clearly, then, the present world economic system is one that presupposes the subjugation of other nations and, more particularly, other races, a system that seems perversely set on maximizing wealth and power regardless of the cost to the society or the environment.[9]

I am not suggesting that the Third World itself is without blame. Let us not, in sentimental manner, deny each other our guilt. The most refined Western paternalism is in fact the one that declares that all faults and problems in the Third World are caused by the West. Much of the Third World's predicament is, in fact, caused by corruption, senseless prestige projects, expensive bureaucracies, irresponsibly high military expenses, maladministration, and the like. But even when all this has been taken into account, it cannot be denied that much of the misery in the Third World can be traced back to policies emanating from the West. It is not that Westerners experience no suffering and distress. They do; but in the West suffering is being privatized, or at least camouflaged and disguised, as our funeral practices illustrate so eloquently. Third World misery, on the contrary, is public and can easily be paraded on our television screens.

A missionary theology for the West should allow us to look at the plight of the Third World (and the Third World within the First) with compassion, for we believe in a God who wants to liberate humankind from every form of injustice, oppression, fatalism, and alienation. This perspective is fundamental to the Christian faith. Already, says Gregory Baum (1991:8), there are Catholic ecclesiastics (and most certainly also Protestant ones!) who argue that the church's reading of the gospel as a call for social justice and solidarity with the poor is based on specifically "modern" presuppositions — presuppositions, that is, that are no longer applicable in this, the postmodern, era. And there can be little doubt that some manifestations of postmodern theory, for instance the writings of Lyotard, seem to point in this direction: if there are no meta-truths, on what would we base our denunciation of the continuation of injustice?

Similar to this kind of apologetic is the attempt to depict evil as a third person reality, as something that is being done, but for which nobody can be held responsible. Its classical formulation is in the thesis that society may be evil but that humans are good. It is strange that this heresy still crops up again and again, after Reinhold Niebuhr, in his *Moral Man and Immoral Society* ([1932] 1960), had so thoroughly exposed the self-confident rationalism of the secularists, the self-confident dialectical materialism of the revolutionaries, and the holier-than-thou pseudo-innocence of the Christians.

In fact, only Christians who know, or should know, about the reality of sin are properly armed against this kind of fallacy. And it is part of our missionary ministry to articulate this in no uncertain terms. Referring to the collapse of the Marxist-Leninist social revolution and its command economy, Charles West writes perceptively:

> This means that the struggle of the poor, the exploited, and victims of the production process have been deprived of an admittedly ambiguous power resource. What will replace it? How will the power balance, now so decisively tipped in favor of the rich and the technologically advanced, be redressed? ... [We] have been deprived of an economic model which claimed to realize justice and equality in an effective system of production and distribution. The model did not work, but it was for years the only one available. Capitalist economists made no serious effort to deal with the justice question. Now we must create new models which are both moral and practical. What form should they take? (1991:440).

Is it then not part and parcel of our Christian *missionary* responsibility to reflect and speak on these questions? And can we not do it much more credibly, without fear of suspicion that we are fifth columnists, now that the Marxist system has collapsed? Is this not the opportunity to rephrase the false questions of Marxism and probe for better answers? West recognizes that Christians have no pat answers to questions like these. But he adds that we have a promise that Marxists never had. Starting with the certainty that the crucified Savior is also the risen Lord, he says:

> We can wade into the human struggle with our gospel of hope, side with the victims, find ways to confront, influence, modify and make responsible the powers

around us, suggest structures of greater justice and human compassion, and above all, let others know who the Lord of the struggle is. This, too, is a form of mission to our culture (1991:441).

God-talk in an Age of Reason

The last quotation from Charles West has already introduced another theme for a missiology of Western culture — faith in God. It may appear trite to introduce this as an item for Western missiology. Still, in light of what was said in the first two parts of this volume about the intrinsically atheistic nature of the Enlightenment and the fact that, apparently, it has made God and faith in God expendable, it is a subject we must address.

By the middle of the nineteenth century the inappropriateness of religion appeared evident to many people. Its imminent demise was widely announced and expected. For Nietzsche, the "death of God," inevitable as it was according to him, was nevertheless an unparalleled catastrophe; it meant that human beings were free-falling into the abyss, but he felt that he had to resign himself to it. According to Freud, religion was surviving in his time simply because the battle of the scientific spirit against religious worldviews had not yet come to its end; religion is, in any case, merely an illusion. Some students of Fichte and Hegel discussed completely dispassionately the question "whether Christianity would survive another twenty or perhaps fifty years" (Lübbe 1986:129). Religion was, after all, only a placebo, and sooner or later people would discover that it makes no difference (:219–28). Marx, by contrast, looked forward with glee to the death of religion. He believed that the progressive change in people's material conditions would, sooner or later, cause belief in a creator god to die a natural death, because it is in any case vacuous. But he went further: because religion is "the opiate of the people," everything possible should be done to remove the conditions that make it necessary.

By the middle of the twentieth century it began to look as if these conditions had been met. Guardini (1950:101) and Polanyi (1958:266) remarked that people were beginning to lose their "natural religious organ," their "capacity to accept any explicit statement of ... belief." Guardini (1950: 112) looked forward to a period when irreligion would become more brazen and described it as a time when the air would be filled with "hostility and danger, but pure and open." He lamented that "without the religious dimension, life becomes like a motor running without oil: it seizes up" (:112), but he appeared helpless to do anything about it.

Even theologians joined in the debate. In the 1960s a widely publicized school of theology proclaimed "the decline of the sacred" and "the death of God." Dietrich Bonhoeffer's statements about "a humanity come of age" and the need for living "as if there were no God" (*etsi deus non daretur*) were preached even from pulpits. Harvey Cox baptized secular society in *The Secular City* (1965). And so on. . . .

Then a strange thing happened. The charismatic movement burst on the scene not among sectarian groups or among the unsophisticated, but in dignified mainline churches like the Roman Catholic and the Anglican, and often among intellectuals, the very products of Enlightenment scientism. Today religion is once more evaluated positively. The so-called religionless world, so it seems, is profoundly religious. Science and religion, in the modern era viewed as incommensurable and irreconcilable, first made a truce, and subsequently science began to open itself to the religious dimension. "Religion has once again become presentable, fit for society and for reasoned discussion," says Manfred Josuttis (1988:16: "*'Religion' is wieder hof- und salon- und diskussionsfähig geworden*"). As the events in Eastern Europe and the former Soviet Union reveal, neither atheistic humanism (à la Feuerbach), nor atheistic socialism (à la Marx), nor atheistic science succeeded in superseding religion (Küng 1990:68). And some twenty years after *The Secular City*, its author declares: "The world of declining religion to which my earlier book was addressed has begun to change in ways that few people anticipated.... Rather than an age of rampant secularization and religious decline, it appears to be more of an era of religious revival and the return of the sacral" (Cox 1984:20). So he wrote a new book, this time about "the unexpected return of religion as a potent social force in a world many thought was leaving it behind," adding that "the task of postmodern theology is to interpret the Christian message at a time when the rebirth of religion, rather than its disappearance, poses the most serious questions" (ibid.). There is, apparently, "more God than we think" (see the title of Maas 1989).

It is not easy to explain this phenomenon. Is it perhaps that the historical conditions for the demise of religion had not yet been met but will still be met at some future date? No, says Lübbe, it is not religion that proved to be an illusion, but the theory of religion that treated it as such (1986:14). Socialism, even if it has developed to full-fledged communism, will never reach the point where it will indisputably have dislodged religion (:129f). The questions to which the critics of religion sought to give answers were formulated wrongly, therefore their answers were equally inappropriate. As a matter of fact, the criticism of religion was fundamentally misplaced.

What we discover again, then, is that the human being is *homo religiosus.* Harvey Cox (1984:13) talks about "some artesian religious quality," "some subcutaneous spirituality" that seems to persist in people. No nonreligious society has ever been found anywhere in the world, and there is no culture that is not profoundly influenced by religious premises (Lübbe 1986:18). The believer is not therefore the aberration, but the so-called modern nonbeliever. Such a person simply does not exist, and those who thought they were nonbelievers were simply suffering from a delusion. The twentieth century Grand Ideologies, as I have argued earlier, are nothing but ersatz religions and faith systems, as is Enlightenment scientism. But they are also pseudo-religions in that they cannot, in the long run, hold the place that belongs to authentic religion. Genuine religion can therefore help us to become resistant to the lure of ideologies; it can be a means of neutralizing ideologies and of making people insusceptible to delusion and immune to their creeds (:63), for authentic religion is no senseless "waiting for Godot."

This does not suggest that we should applaud every form of contemporary religious revival. Much of it is indeed spurious. New Age, esoterics, astrology, magic, neo-gnostic occultism, and the like revel in the pluralistic culture of postmodernism but are often merely atavistic manifestations of earlier worldviews like gnosticism, mysticism, theosophy, and romanticism. Precisely the fact that they fit easily into the contemporary climate without causing a ripple on the surface should make us wary. Authentic religion, says Josuttis (1988:17), endangers the emerging postmodern worldview. With the easy integration of religion into its system, it has swallowed a poison that it will find hard to digest (:16). The biblical faith, however, contains elements that are much more intractable and antagonistic to the new worldview than may be expected (:19). Faith in the one God who revealed himself in Jesus Christ does not fit into the pluralistic postmodern order (Daecke 1988:630; Baum 1991:7).

What does all this mean for a missiology of Western culture? I believe it means that we can indeed be more bold and confident than we tend to be in the face of what we judge to be an omnipresent (and omnipotent?) irreligiosity. This irreligiosity is a myth and should be exposed as such. People worship gods, even if they do not know it or deny it vehemently. We have to proclaim to them that there is no other god but God and that they should worship no "foreign" gods. This was the pristine confession of Israel, flowing from the experience of the Exodus. The analogous confession of the New Testament church flowed from its encounter with the crucified and risen Christ, an experience that relativized all Jewish signs and all Greek wisdom. It empowered them to wager on something fundamentally different from the conventional religiously legitimated state of affairs (Maas 1991:8–10, 14). The Christian missionary of today either shares in that same experience or is no Christian missionary. On the basis of that, the missionary can proclaim the living God to one's contemporaries, seeking the searchers, providing new roots to the uprooted, caring for those who do not care, giving direction to those who, in a despair they are not consciously aware of, live by the horoscope, and gently touching the deeper stirrings in the hearts of those who sense that what they enjoy today cannot be all there is, those who seek after "the spiritual dimension of life" and "an antidote to dehumanization" (*Redemptoris Missio* 38).

This presupposes a catharsis of the church, too, however. By and large, the revival of religion is not evident in the mainline churches and their Sunday services. It manifests itself outside Christianity or in groups outside the historical churches, or, alternatively, in the nontraditional activities of these churches, such as *Kirchentage*.[10] Frequently our churches are empty not because the Christian faith is unacceptable to the modern world, but because of the "counter-witness of believers and Christian communities failing to follow the model of Christ" (*Redemptoris Missio* 36). In many respects our track record is against us.

5

The Impossibility of Not Believing

We have to look at the theme just discussed from yet another angle.

Enlightenment scientism has taught people that the acceptance of unproven beliefs was the broad road to darkness. Only universal doubt would purge the human mind of all opinions held merely on trust and open it to knowledge firmly grounded in reason. We should keep our minds empty rather than allow any but irrefutable beliefs to take possession of them. Only along this straight and narrow path would we arrive at an unassailable residue of knowledge that is completely determined by objective evidence (Polanyi: 1958:269).

Because of the growing dislike of what was perceived to be religious bigotry, this Enlightenment tenet of the efficacy of doubt as a solvent of error was increasingly aimed specifically at religion, at faith (:279). It has been an extraordinarily successful teaching. It has become the "received view"; and all of us, when we are told of something we had not known of before, respond spontaneously: "Where is your proof? What are the facts?" Even Polanyi, who set out systematically to refute this approach, acknowledges that he, too, finds ingrained in his own mind the notion that to refrain from believing unproven assertions is always an act of intellectual honesty and that to believe them is to throw oneself wide open to the suspicion of obscurantism (:271f). What one had to aim at was total objectivity.

Today most disciplines, including the natural sciences, concede — albeit grudgingly at times — that this view was based on an illusion, that there is no such thing as complete objectivity, and that a host of factors codetermine our convictions. The problem is, however, that most of the people in our streets, offices, factories, and schools do not seem to be aware of the monumental shift that has taken place during the past thirty years or so. They still live and act as if the tenets of scientific objectivity are completely intact and indisputable. We have a major missionary task in this respect, a task that may turn out to be even more difficult than the other ones I have outlined above.

What is it that we have to communicate to the Western "post-Christian" public? It seems to me that we must demonstrate the role that plausibility structures, or, rather, worldviews, play in people's lives. This is best illustrated when people undergo a change in worldview, something we may describe, phenomenologically at least, as conversion. We hold our worldviews implicitly; that means we are often not consciously aware of them. However, when they change, we realize something of the grip they used to have on us. Polanyi (1958:288) gives two quotations to illustrate this: one from Arthur Koestler, a former Marxist (from his important book *The God that Failed*); the other from Karen Horney, a former Freudian. Although still adhering to Marxism or Freudianism, they would have regarded the all-embracing interpretative powers of Marxism's or Freudianism's framework as evidence of its truth; only when losing faith in it did they feel that its powers were specious. From this perspective, then, we may deduce that those who swore by rationalism as the only position one could embrace with integrity had actually undergone a conversion: from faith in God to faith in their independent rational faculties.

Worldviews are integrative and interpretive frameworks by which order and disorder are judged, they are the standards by which reality is managed and pursued, sets of hinges on which all our everyday thinking and doing turns (Olthuis 1991:4f). Worldviews are, of course, formed by several factors. It is not true as some religious fundamentalists like to argue that one's worldview is shaped solely by one's faith or by God. Worldviews are shaped by both inculcated (or assumed) faith convictions *and* by context, social status, emotional health, and the like. They are shaped by both "theory" and "practice," which condition each other, or, in Christian parlance, by both divine revelation and human experience.[11] A worldview, moreover, functions both descriptively (it tells us what is or what is not the case) and normatively (it tells us what might or ought not to be the case). It is both a sketch of and a blueprint for reality, a vision *of* life and *for* life (:5).

The significance of all of this is critical. As a vision rooted in faith (*any* kind of faith) *and* experience, a worldview in its basic tenets is not argued *to*, but argued *from* (:8). It is not the terminus of our quest for insight, but our place of departure. This is the point Polanyi (1958:266) intends to make when he again holds up the Augustinian (and Anselmian) adage: *Nisi credideritis non intelligitis* ("unless you believe, you shall not understand"). Apparently, Enlightenment scientism has inverted the mutual position of the two Augustinian levels to read: "unless you understand, you shall not believe," but only *apparently,* since scientism also, unwittingly, follows the Augustinian logic: only because it *believes* in the power of unaided reason does it *understand* everything in these terms. It is an illusion that one can follow the other path; it is, moreover, a false ideal (:18). Belief is, in fact, the source of all knowledge (:266).

We move ahead yet another step. According to Polanyi (1958:271), all fundamental beliefs are *irrefutable* as well as *unprovable* — that is, in terms of the axioms of our society — for the test of proof or disproof is irrelevant for the acceptance or rejection of fundamental beliefs. Such a philosophy does not eliminate doubt but, like the Christian faith, says "that we should hold on to what we truly believe, even when realizing the absurdly remote chances of this enterprise, trusting the unfathomable intimations that call upon us to do so" (:313).

Is there then not a danger that our beliefs may be wrong? Alternatively, does this approach not lead us into total subjectivism? I have already referred to the postmodernism of Lyotard and others who, for fear of the first (that our beliefs may be wrong), deny the existence of any meta-truth and meta-narratives against which we may test our convictions, and therefore end in relativism and subjectivism, indeed, in irrationalism. Such irrationalism, says Sigmund Daecke (1988:632), is, however, even more perilous than modern rationalism. And this is certainly not what Polanyi propounds. It is precisely because he believes that we stand "under a firmament of truth and greatness" (:380) and that "the universe is sufficiently intelligible to justify this undertaking" that it is "incumbent upon us to take these chances," as we "draw confidence from the splendor of a thousand minds to which we pay homage" (:318).

The position the believer adopts is therefore not irrational; it is eminently reasonable. After the Enlightenment it is impossible that it could be otherwise. We can now profess "knowingly and openly those beliefs which could be tacitly taken for granted" before the onset of the critical era (:268). We moreover concede that, "in spite of its a-critical character, the force of religious conviction does depend on factual evidence and can be affected by doubt concerning certain facts" (:280). In this respect, Polanyi refers to faith and worship as a "passionate heuristic impulse" or "vision" with the help of which we continually probe the authenticity of our faith.

It follows from this that Christian theology can be pursued only from the basis of such a faith commitment. In this process it will, surely, make use of rational discourse, even if it will never identify itself with reason (Hoedemaker 1990:62). Theological enquiry is not the *fruit* of faith, not the means by which to arrive at faith. Faith can only be "caught," not taught. Theology can, however, be a critical instrument in helping us to cleanse the fountains of our faith. We live in a time in which new forms must be found and new linkages forged between faith and rationality; perhaps the present "god-less" time is really a creative transition period (:59). Theologizing can therefore and, if it is done properly, will lead to change in my worldview or frame of reference, because this is always, of necessity, deficient. It will not, however, answer all questions. Because people have been taught by the rationalist system that all questions can, in principle, find answers, they have sometimes become exasperated with the loose ends of their thinking and have changed over to another system, heedless of similar difficulties within that new system (Polanyi 1958:18). The sense of inadequacy of our heuristic impulse is, however, part of the Christian faith: "its striving can never reach an endpoint at which having gained its desired result, its continuation would become unnecessary" (:280). Our theology can never "put at our disposal what cannot, by definition, be at our disposal" (Lübbe 1986:16). A sense of imperfection is essential to the Christian faith. Polanyi quotes Tillich in support of this view: "Faith embraces itself and the doubt about itself" (:280).

It thus remains *my* vision, *our* vision; but if it compels my allegiance, should it not do the same for others? If not, why do I believe? What we believe to be most true for ourselves, we must also implicitly believe to be worth the commitment of others and explicitly communicate to them (Olthuis 1991:13). It is, after all, a faith we hold "with universal intent" (Polanyi).

Should we not, then, incorporate this vision of a faith that is unprovable and yet real to our contemporaries as well? Should we not go out of our way to expose the flimsy foundations on which their rationalism, materialism, or what have you stand? Is this not part of our missionary (and therefore missiological) agenda? And what would happen if we do not communicate such a worldview to them? What would they be left with? What would be their lodestar, the contents of their hopes, yes, of what they *believe*? Let Polanyi reply to these questions:

Then law is no more than what the courts will decide, art but an emollient of nerves, morality but a convention, tradition but an inertia, God but a psychological necessity. Then man dominates a world in which he himself does not exist. For with his obligations he has lost his voice and his hope, and been left behind meaningless to himself (1958:380).

6

Conclusion

I have discussed five ingredients of a missiology of Western culture. I have singled these out because I believe them to be of crucial importance. They are not the only elements needed. There are others as well, but because they are of a more general nature or involve less complex issues, a few sentences about each of them will have to suffice.

1. A missiology of Western culture must include an *ecological* dimension. The time is long past that we can afford to exclude the environment from our missionary agenda. It was because of this conviction that the Southern African Missiological Society decided to devote its 1991 Annual Congress to the theme of "Mission and Ecology." To the surprise of the organizers, they received more offers for papers than for any of the Society's twenty-two previous congresses — a clear indication that missionaries and missiologists have begun to wake up to this important dimension of their ministry. For mission to the West, this theme is of crucial importance not only because of the ecological threats in the West itself, but also because, first, it was the West, with its technology and mechanistic worldview, that led in the subjugation and exploitation of nature in the first place;

second, it has become clear that the earth cannot survive if all were to live the way people in developed countries live; and third, the current exploitation of the environment in the Third World (for instance, the disappearance of the Brazilian rain forests and the damage to the ozone layer) is often directly linked to the global economic structure that is dictated by the West (Müller 1990:514–16).

The political and liberation theologies of recent decades understood themselves in terms of overcoming the subjectivist, individualist, and existentialist reduction of theology. Only recently did we begin to add to our theological agenda our responsibility in respect of the environment agenda, as illustrated particularly in the ecumenical Justice, Peace, and the Integrity of Creation project (JPIC). The "justice and peace" part is wholeheartedly supported by the churches of the Third World. There is more ambivalence, though, about the "integrity of creation" part, as was illustrated by the JPIC Conference that met in Seoul in 1989. On the one hand they suspect it to be a ploy of Western Christians to deemphasize the priority of justice; on the other, they believe that, in any case, the West is far more guilty than they are when it comes to ruining the environment.

It will, I believe, be impossible to develop a credible missiology of Western culture without paying serious attention to these issues and without an articulate witness in this respect to those in the West we hope to reach.

2. It follows from the previous point that a mission to the West must be *countercultural*, though not in an escapist way. The point is that Western culture, perhaps due to Locke's philosophy, is inherently hedonistic, emphasizing the selfish dimension in human nature. Bacon said that the goal of science was "to ease man's estate"; Descartes said

that science will make us "masters and possessors of nature." This mentality has injected into our culture an insatiable desire for self-gratification. People want to enjoy their football matches, rock festivals, television programs, holidays, and parties — all of which they "deserve" after a hard day's work. Sacrifice, asceticism, modesty, self-discipline, and the like, are not popular virtues. Much of this has entered into our churches as well, tangibly in the "prosperity gospel," more effectively camouflaged in mainline churches but present there as well (Bellah 1991:469f). We all crave for acceptance by our culture and for a well-defined role within it. But then the gospel becomes inoffensive and inoperable, with Christianity just another societal element. I believe that we have to communicate an alternative culture to our contemporaries. Part of our mission will be to challenge the hedonism around us, inculcating something of the spirit of being "resident aliens" in the world (Hauerwas and Willimon 1989, 1991).

3. A mission to the West will have to be *ecumenical.* This implies, at the very least, an explicitly critical attitude toward denominationalism, something we not only invented for ourselves but also exported to the ends of the earth. Bellah (1991:463) points out that denominationalism, particularly in the United States, descends from the Lockean contract model; it generated consumer Christians who shop around among churches for the best package deal they can get. Newbigin concurs. He reminds us

that denominationalism is the religious aspect of secularization. It is the form that religion takes in a culture controlled by the ideology of the Enlightenment. It is the social form in which the privatization of religion is expressed (1986:145).

Now if there is any truth in this, we cannot, now that we are moving into a postmodern era, simply take along this albatross around our necks as if nothing has happened. Thank God, there are gratifying indications that in our missionary involvement in many parts of the world we are indeed taking seriously the rediscovered reality of our fundamental unity (Bosch 1991:457–67). There are, however, also disturbing indications to the contrary, not only in Protestantism, but also in some recent statements emanating from the Vatican. But mission to the West dare not be recruitment to our brand of religion not only because the task before us is too immense to be credibly and effectively tackled by a fragmented church, but because the very nature of mission militates against this kind of ecclesiastical empire building. Mission is, rather, the communication of the good news about the universal and coming reign of the true and living God.

4. We have, at long last, come to the conviction that mission in the Third World must be *contextual*. We do not have an equally clear conviction about the need for contextualization in the West. Somehow we still believe that the gospel has already been (has always been?) properly indigenized and contextualized in the West. However, as we now know, the West has largely turned its back on the gospel. Was it perhaps because the gospel was never properly contextualized? Or perhaps overcontextualized, so much so that it has lost its distinctive character and challenge? What, indeed, will contextualization of the gospel in the West involve and look like? I submit that we do not really know.

That makes it all the more necessary to reflect on this issue with the utmost urgency.

5. A missionary encounter with the West will have to be, primarily, a ministry of the *laity*. The professionalization of the ordained ministry has an ancient history, going back to the early centuries of the Christian church. The Protestant Reformation rediscovered the office of the believer; however, in the main branches of the Reformation churches this remained largely theoretical. Only in the Radical Reformation did it really take root, but even the churches emanating from this branch of the Reformation have today largely professionalized the ordained ministry. For our present theme the revitalization of the office of the believer is crucial, for two reasons: first, the church's witness will be much more credible if it comes from those who do not belong to the guild of pastors; and second, only in this way will we begin to bring together what our culture has divided, the private and the public, for the lay members of the church clearly belong to the public and secular world, whereas the pastors belong to a separate, "religious" world (Newbigin 1986:143).

6. I have to take this one step further: in the context of the secularized, post-Christian West our witness will be credible only if it flows from a *local, worshiping community*. Newbigin (1989:222–33) suggests that the only hermeneutic of the gospel is a congregation of men and women who believe it and live by it. I am deeply indebted to Michael Polanyi. At one point, however, I have to criticize him: he seems to have no eye for the *community* as bearer of the faith. He almost exclusively uses the first person singular. He seems to be unaware of the extent to which he has, in this respect, internalized and succumbed to the individual-

ism of the Enlightenment. However, unlike philosophical schools or scientific experiments, theology has no life unless it is borne by a community. The same is true of mission. Thus the question about the feasibility of a missionary enterprise to Western people hinges on the question of the nature and life of our local worshiping communities and the extent to which they facilitate a discourse in which the engagement of people with their culture is encouraged. Local church "happens" where believers are involved in what is critical for people and society (Hoedemaker 1990:64f). It is not, however, as though we still have to *invent* this community (that would be the "sectarian," or separatist, solution). As Hauerwas and Willimon (1989; 1991:424) put it, what we want already exists: "Christians are sitting on a gold mine called the church, but unfortunately the very categories we have been taught as Western Christians make it difficult for us to notice that it is gold."

I conclude. Even if we take seriously all the dimensions and ingredients outlined above, we will have no guarantees of success. God does not ask about the extent of our successes, however; rather, we are asked about the depth of our commitment. We do not know what the future holds. Writing in the wake of the Second World War, Guardini suggested that the fundamental problem in the future would be that of *power*. The first wilderness, nature, had been domesticated. Power, the second wilderness, would not be so easily subdued. He added:

> All monsters of the deserts, all demons of darkness are here again. Once again people stand face to face with chaos; and what makes it so much more terrible is the fact that the majority do not compre-

hend what is at hand. For everywhere scientifically informed people are conversing, machines are running, and bureaucracies are functioning (1950:96; my translation).

Much later (1982:275) Johannes Aagaard expressed similar sentiments. The soft age of mission, he suggested, had gone. "The days of the *missio triumfans* have passed and the days of the *missio pressa* have come.... The decisive missiological questions to which we have to respond will often be put to us by the judges and the prosecutors." Along with Matthew 28, Matthew 10 would now be "the charter for missiological praxis and reflection."

In the present climate, after the momentous political events of 1991 and with the dawn of a so-called New World Order, the words of Guardini and Aagaard sound strangely unreal, even apocalyptic. They scarcely seem to have any bearing on mission in the Third World, let alone in the West. Here, the greatest danger for our missionary ministry appears to be that it may be sovereignly ignored. And yet, the situation could change rapidly and unexpectedly. Whatever the future might be, our missionary task will remain. Let us prepare ourselves for it.

Notes

1. It is hard to know whether American Christians were deriving their status from those forms of political power valued by the wider culture or whether it happened the other way round. Hauerwas muses, "It is unclear who started looking like who first, whether Southern Baptist pastors started looking like Texas politicians, or Texas politicians started looking like Southern Baptist pastors!" (Hauerwas and Willimon 1991:422).

2. I am using Niebuhr's taxonomy with some reservations and simply because no better taxonomy has so far been produced — something that is direly needed. I agree with Hunsberger (1991:406, note 1) that the categories of Niebuhr's paradigm fail to account for the complexities involved in the relationship between Christian faith and culture and for the evolving configurations of Western culture. Cf. also Hauerwas and Willimon 1989 and 1991:426.

3. Küng (1990:179, note 35) appropriately criticizes Sölle (1990: 6–18) for reducing all of Protestant theology to a simple scheme of orthodox versus liberal.

4. From an analogous point of view, the Dutch theologian A. A. van Ruler has adopted a similar position: God has had a history with Western people unlike the history God has had with other peoples, and this has left an indelible mark on Western humanity.

5. Cf. Friedrich Engel's essay *Die Entwicklungdes Sozialismus von der Utopie zur Wissenschaft* (1882).

6. See, in this respect, the "scientific" studies published in Nazi Germany and South Africa in the area of *Rassenkunde* (Lübbe 1986:66).

7. As such they are, in the words of Raymond Aron, *L'opium des intellectuels* (Lübbe 1986:63, note 31).

8. Küng (1990:43) is correct, however, when he argues that these views are not to be regarded as characteristic of postmodernity; rather, they are manifestations of the disintegrated late-modern era.

9. Neither is this a new issue. Two decades ago already the then West German minister of Economic Cooperation, Erhard Eppler, published a booklet with the title *Not Much Time for the Third World.*

10. Lübbe 1986:130, note 30, reports that up to 140,000 young people attended some sessions of the German Catholic *Kirchentag* held in Munich in 1984.

11. The multidimensional origin and nature of a worldview should caution us not to absolutize or canonize it. Neither, for that matter, should one minimize it. If we do canonize our worldview or if we adopt a static worldview, the development of faith and of insight in the light of faith is stopped cold (cf. Olthuis 1991:4, 12).

References Cited

Aagaard, Johannes. 1982. The Soft Age Has Gone. *Missiology* 10: 263–77.

Barth, Karl. 1956. *Church Dogmatics IV/1*. Edinburgh: T & T Clark.

Baum, Gregory. 1979. *The Social Imperative: Essays on the Critical Issues that Confront the Christian Churches*. New York/Ramsey, N.J./Toronto: Paulist Press.

———. 1991. Theories of Post-Modernity. *The Ecumenist* 29:4–12.

Becker, George. 1991. Pietism's Confrontation with Enlightenment Rationalism: An Examination of the Relation Between Ascetic Protestantism and Science. *Journal for the Scientific Study of Religion* 30:139–58.

Bell, Daniel. 1973. *The Coming of Post-Industrial Society: A Venture in Social Forecasting*. New York: Basic Books.

Bellah, Robert N., et al. 1985. *Habits of the Heart: Individualism and Commitment in American Life*. Berkeley: University of California Press.

———. 1991. Cultural Barriers to the Understanding of the Church and Its Public Role. *Missiology* 19:461–73.

Berkhof, Hendrikus. 1966. *Christ the Meaning of History*. London: SCM Press.

Bernstein, Richard J. 1985. *The Restructuring of Social and Political Theory*. London: Methuen & Co. First published 1976.

Bloom, Allan. 1987. *The Closing of the American Mind*. New York: Simon & Schuster.

Bosch, David J. 1984. Missionary Theology in Africa. *Indian Missiological Review* 6:105–39.

———. 1991. *Transforming Mission: Paradigm Shifts in Theology of Mission*. Maryknoll, N.Y.: Orbis Books.

British Council of Churches. 1980. *Nationwide Initiative in Evangelism.* London: BCC.

Chalmers, A. F. 1985. *What Is This Thing Called Science?* Milton Keynes, Bucks., Eng.: Open University Press. 2d edition.

Church of England. 1918. *Committee of Enquiry into the Evangelistic Work of the Church.* London.

Cox, Harvey. 1966. *The Secular City: Secularization and Urbanization in Theological Perspective.* Harmondsworth, Eng.: Penguin. First published 1965.

———. 1984. *Religion in the Secular City: Toward a Postmodern Theology.* New York: Simon & Schuster.

Daecke, Sigmund M. 1988. Glaube im Pluralismus: Gibt es eine post-moderne Theologie? *Evangelische Kommentare* 21:629–32.

Eberlein, Gerard L. 1991. Was heisst heute Aufklärung? Neue Antworten auf eine alte Frage. *Evangelische Kommentare* 24: 541–43.

Eppler, Erhard. 1972. *Not Much Time for the Third World.* London: Oswald Wolff.

Farley, Edward. 1983. *Theologia: The Fragmentation and Unity of Theological Education.* Philadelphia: Fortress Press.

Fensham, C. J. 1990. Missiology for the Future: Developing a Missiology in the Light of the Emerging Systemic Paradigm. Ph.D. diss., University of South Africa, Pretoria.

Feyerabend, Paul. 1975. *Against Method: An Outline of an Anarchistic Theory of Knowledge.* London: New Left Books.

Godin, H., and Y. Daniel. 1943. *France, pays de mission?* Paris: Editions du Cerf.

Grindel, John A., C. M. 1991. *Whither the U.S. Church? Context, Gospel, Planning.* Maryknoll, N.Y.: Orbis Books.

Guardini, Romano. 1950. *Das Ende der Neuzeit.* Wurzburg: Werkbund-Verlag.

Habermas, Jürgen. 1988. *Nachmetaphysisches Denken. Philosophische Aufsatze.* Frankfurt: Suhrkamp.

Hauerwas, Stanley, and William H. Willimon. 1989. *Resident Aliens.* Nashville: Abingdon Press.

———. 1991. Why Resident Aliens Struck a Chord. *Missiology* 19: 419–29.

Hoedemaker, L. A. 1988. Het volk van God en de einden der aarde. *Oecumenische Inleiding in de Missiologie.* Kampen: Kok, 167–80.

———. 1990. Secularisatie, kerk en samenleving. *Wending* 45:54–65.

Horkheimer, M., and T. W. Adorno. 1947. *Dialektik der Aufklärung: Philosophische Fragmente.* Amsterdam: Querido Verlag.

Hunsberger, George R. 1991. The Newbigin Gauntlet: Developing a Domestic Missiology for North America. *Missiology* 19:391–408.

John Paul II. 1990. *Redemptoris Missio.* Vatican City: Libreria Editrice Vaticana.

Josuttis, Manfred. 1988. Religion Gefahr der Postmoderne. *Evangelische Kommentare* 21:16–19.

Kaiser, Christopher. 1991. *Creation and the History of Science.* Grand Rapids: Eerdmans.

Küng, Hans. 1987. *Theologie im Aufbruch: Eine ökumenische Grundlegung.* Munich: Piper Verlag.

———. 1990. *Projekt Weltethos.* Munich/Zurich: Piper Verlag.

Küng, Hans, and David Tracy, eds. 1984. *Theologie wohin? Auf dem Weg zu einem neuen Paradigma.* Zurich-Cologne: Benziger Verlag.

Leegwater, A. 1991. Response to J. J. Venter: "The World: A Machine or a God?" *Reformed Ecumenical Synod Theological Forum* 19:3:33–35.

Lübbe, Hermann. 1986. *Religion nach der Aufklärung.* Graz/Vienna/Cologne: Verlag Styria.

Lyotard, J.-F. 1986. *The Postmodern Condition.* Manchester: Manchester University Press.

Maas, Frans. 1989. *Er is meer God dan wij denken.* Kampen: Kok.

———. 1991. Een nieuwe kans voor 'negatieve theologie'? *Wending* 46:7–15.

Margull, H. J. 1962. *Hope in Action: The Church's Task in the World.* Philadelphia: Muhlenberg Press.

Mette, Norbert. 1990. Vom Säkularisierungs — zum Evangelisierungsparadigma. *Diakonia: Internationale Zeitschrift für die Praxis der Kirche* 21:420–29.

Müller, Johannes, S.J. 1990. Europa Festung des Wohlstands gegen die Dritte Welt? Herausforderungen an die Entwicklungspolitik der 90er Jahre. *Stimmen der Zeit* 115:507–20.

Nationwide Initiative in Evangelism. 1980. *Evangelism: Convergence and Divergence.* London: Nationwide Initiative in Evangelism.

Neill, Stephen C. 1968. *The Church and Christian Union.* London: Oxford University Press.

Nel, D. T. 1989. Kritiese Hermeneutiek as model vir sending-wetenskaplike navorsing. Ph.D. diss., University of South Africa, Pretoria.

Newbigin, Lesslie. 1986. *Foolishness to the Greeks: The Gospel and Western Culture.* Geneva: World Council of Churches.

———. 1989. *The Gospel in a Pluralist Society.* Grand Rapids: Eerdmans.

Niebuhr, H. Richard. 1956. *Christ and Culture.* New York: Harper & Brothers. First published 1951.

Niebuhr, Reinhold. 1960. *Moral Man and Immoral Society.* New York: Charles Scribner's Sons. First published 1932.

Olthuis, James H. 1991. On Worldviews. *Reformed Ecumenical Synod Theological Forum* 19:3:2–14.

Polanyi, Michael. 1958. *Personal Knowledge: Towards a Post-Critical Philosophy.* London: Routledge & Kegan Paul.

Rahner, Karl. 1966. Grundprinzipien zur heutigen Mission der Kirche. Vol. 2/2 of *Handbuch der Pastoraltheologie.* Freiburg im Breisgau: Herder, 46–80.

———. 1969. Die Zukunft der Kirche hat schon begonnen. Vol. 4 of *Handbuch der Pastoraltheologie.* Freiburg im Breisgau: Herder, 744–59.

Shenk, Wilbert R. 1991. Missionary Encounter with Culture. *International Bulletin of Missionary Research* 15:104–9.

Sölle, Dorothee. 1990. *Thinking About God: An Introduction to Theology.* Valley Forge, Pa.: Trinity Press International.

Tillich, Paul. 1951. *The Protestant Era.* London: James Nisbet & Co.

Touraine, Alain. 1977. *The Self-Production of Society.* Chicago: University of Chicago Press.

Vanackere, Hans. 1990. How Shall They Believe? *Mission Outlook* 22:105–8.

Verkuyl, J. 1978. *Inleiding in de evangelistiek.* Kampen: Kok.
West, Charles C. 1991. Gospel for American Culture: Variations on a Theme by Newbigin. *Missiology: An International Review* 19: 431–41.
Wolterstorff, Nicholas. 1983. *Until Justice and Peace Embrace.* Grand Rapids: Eerdmans.

Lightning Source UK Ltd.
Milton Keynes UK
UKOW04f1039220216

268854UK00001B/14/P